Reading and Comprehending

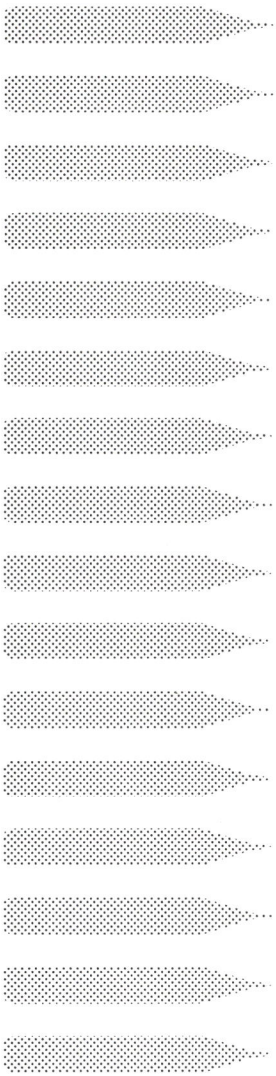

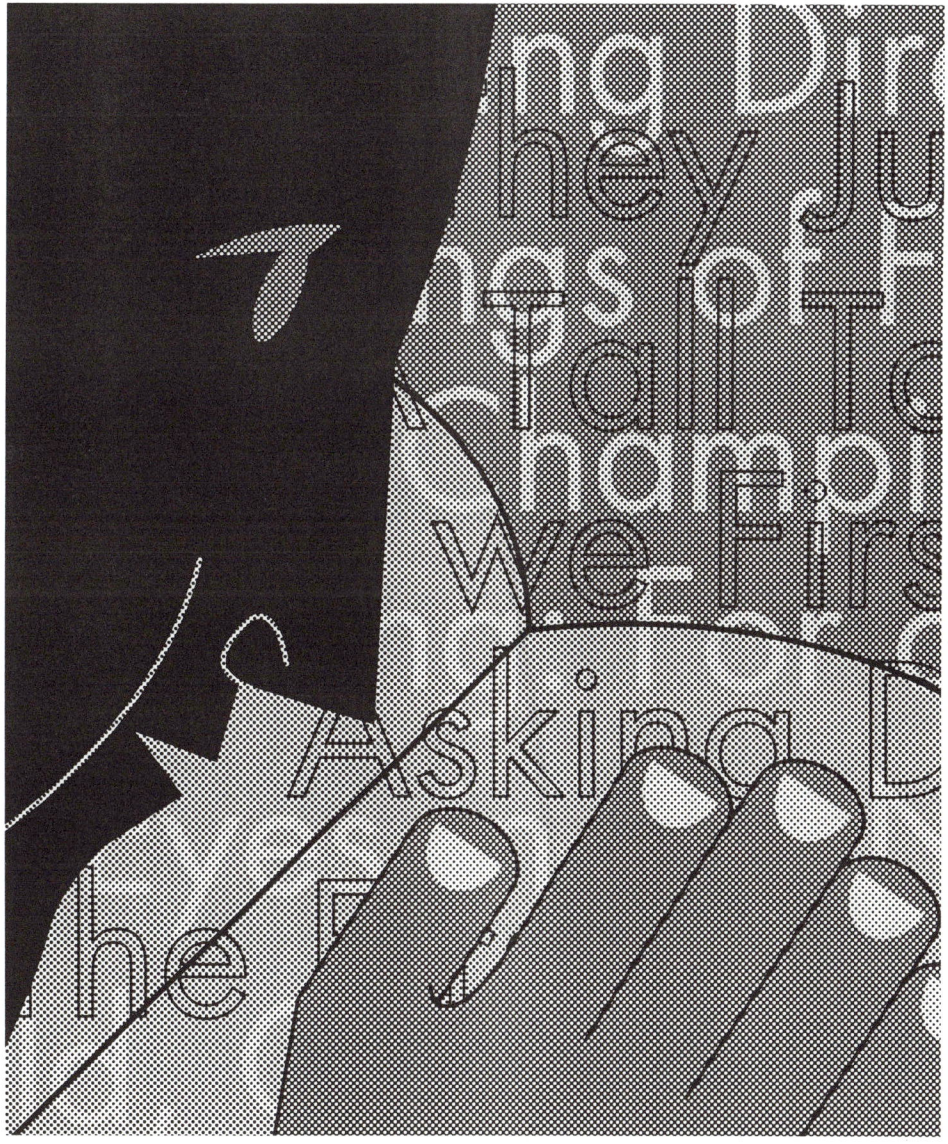

Diane Henderson and Bruce Tuffin

Prim-Ed Publishing

Foreword and Contents

Reading and Comprehending is a copymaster compiled specifically for the revision of fundamental skills. The concepts introduced and developed here are those normally introduced in early stages of learning (8-12 years), but have been produced in a manner that meets the needs of adolescent and adult learners. These learners may require remedial work, revision or could be being introduced to the English language. Page layout and artwork has been designed to compliment the needs of a mature learner, while maintaining the basic simplicity of fundamental language development skills.

Note: this book is a compilation adapted from the series 'Comprehend It!'.

Introduction

Reading and Comprehending copymasters are designed to present the accepted levels of comprehension to students, in an attractive format, using original and interesting writing, both fiction and non-fiction.

The artwork used is not just for 'decoration', although visual appeal is an important factor in boosting motivation; it has been drawn to assist the students in their understanding of the written material.

To assist teachers while remaining unobtrusive to students, the comprehension exercises on each worksheet have been coded, using the following code:

Level A   =   Literal
Level B   =   Interpretative
Level C   =   Evaluative

A = green
B = amber
C = red

(While some syllabuses do in fact promote four lev___ ___he writers' contention that the two final categories un___ ___ happily placed together as 'Evaluative'.)

Levels of Comprehension

Modern approaches to teaching comprehension recognize the need for students to be able to comprehend more than in a literal form: and now look to develop the student's ability to make inferences from the text and accompanying art, and then also form opinions from their reading. The main levels of comprehension are explained below.

Literal

Literal questions require a specific literal answer where all information is provided in the text or the art. This is the traditional form of questioning and is asking students to take literal meaning from the text, without any interpretation or opinion.
For example, the question may read "What colour was the boat?". The answer can only be provided as a specific colour, such as "The boat was green"

Inferential

Inferential questions require inferences to be made based on partial information provided in the text. These questions require the student to collect what information that is available and then infer an answer from this.
For example, the question may be "Who was at the door?". The text provides the information that there was a scratching sound at the door. A valid inference and answer may be "The cat was at the door".

Evaluative

Evaluative questions require the student to make a judgement based on information in the text and their own opinion/s. Also included in this form of questions are appreciative questions which require the student to show an understanding of the author's intent and any hidden messages. When providing opinions and judgements students should be encouraged to support their opinions with explanations.

A Little Bit Wild

There is something special about a cat. It is its own boss. It takes no orders from anyone. A cat will only do something if it *wants* to do it. No matter how tame it might be, a cat still *seems* to be a little bit wild.

Cats were first tamed in Egypt about 3 500 years ago. They were very special animals to the Egyptians. We have even found old, old statues with the head of a cat and a person's body.

When a cat died, it was sometimes buried in a special 'grave'—with mice for food while going to 'heaven'.

Cats finally spread to Europe. But things were not so good for them there! They were thought to be the pets of witches and a sign of the devil. Thousands of cats were hunted down and killed. It was to take hundreds of years before cats would again be popular as pets.

Today, cats are as popular as dogs for pets. But there is a problem. When cats 'run away' into the wild, they become deadly killers. They destroy many native animals and birds. Cats make great pets, but they are very dangerous if they go wild.

Some unthinking people have kittens because they are fun to play with. But once the kitten grows up, they don't want it any more and just dump it. That poor cat then has to become a hunter to live. That's unfair to the cat and to the animals it hunts.

If you have a kitten, remember it is a pet for life, not just until it grows up!

Level A

1. How long have cats been tamed?

    _____

    _____

2. Why were mice put in a cat's tomb after it died?

    _____

3. What do some people do with cats they don't want?

    _____

    _____

4. What is so 'special' about cats?

    _____

    _____

Level B

1. What did the ancient Egyptians think of cats?

    _____

2. Why is it unfair to dump kittens or cats?

    _____

    _____

3. Why were thousands of cats killed in Europe?

    _____

    _____

4. How can cats be a danger to the environment?

    _____

    _____

    _____

    _____

Level C

1. Why does a cat always seem to be 'a little bit wild'?

_____

_____

2. What does the writer mean by saying a cat 'is a pet for life'?

_____

_____

3. Draw a picture of what you think the Egyptian statue with a cat's head and a human body might look like.

Old, Old Insects

No matter where you go in the world, you will find cockroaches. These insects have been around for over 300 million years! Cockroach fossils are still found today in coal and rock. They tell us that cockroaches were on the earth before dinosaurs, before birds, before humans! And they haven't changed very much since then.

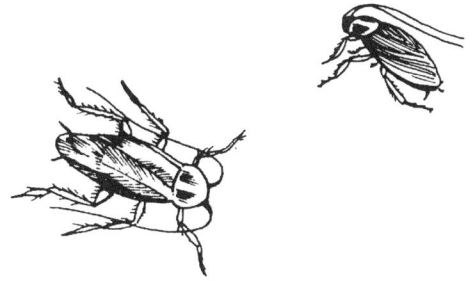

There are many reasons why cockroaches have lasted so long. Here are some of them:

- Most of them can fly.
- They can make themselves flat to sneak in anywhere.
- They can go from stopped to full speed faster than a sports car.
- They are *very* hard to kill.

Cockroaches can also eat just about anything. For example, apart from food scraps or rotting plants, they can eat paper, glue, plastics, shoe polish and even human fingernail clippings! Because they can go from rotting rubbish to human food, they can also spread diseases and make people very ill.

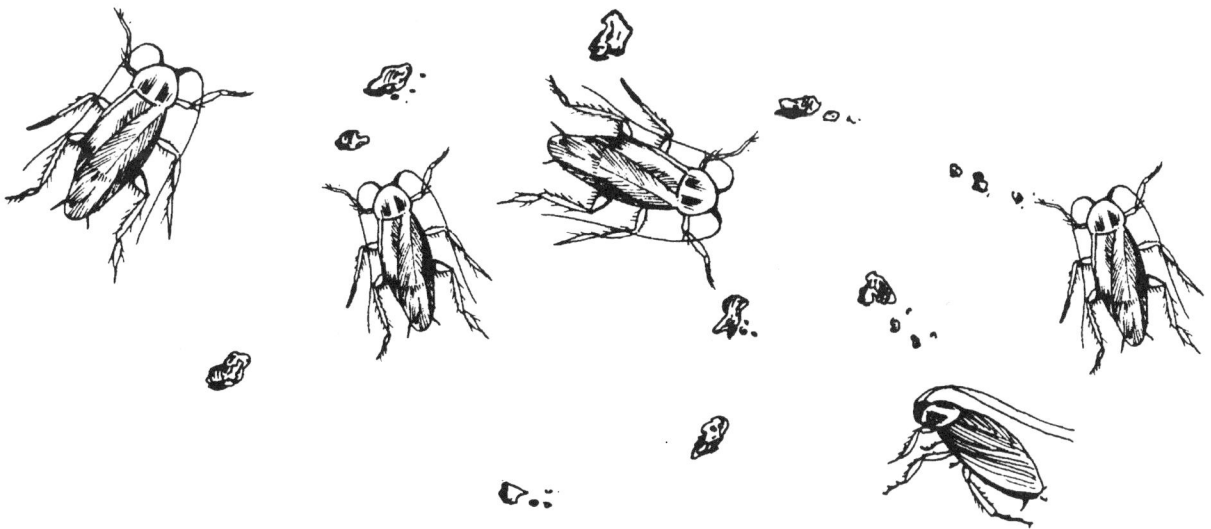

Cockroaches are thought of as a pest. Each year, people spend billions of pounds around the world trying to get rid of cockroaches. Sadly, the poisons they use often do more damage to *useful* insects and animals than they do to cockroaches.

Humans will probably never get rid of cockroaches, but they will keep on trying! In millions of years from now, humans might be gone from the earth. But it's a safe bet there will still be cockroaches!

Level A

1. Where can you find cockroach fossils?

    _____

    _____

2. How long have cockroaches been on the earth?

    _____

    _____

3. What do cockroaches eat?

    _____

4. Give four reasons why cockroaches have lasted so long?

    _____

    _____

    _____

    _____

Level B

1. Which came first: humans or cockroaches?

    _____

2. Who would *lose* money if cockroaches suddenly died out? Why?

    _____

    _____

3. Why are cockroaches thought of as a pest?

    _____

    _____

    _____

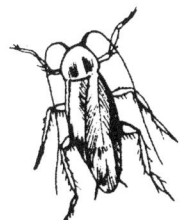

Level C

1. Why haven't cockroaches changed very much in 300 million years?

    _____

    _____

2. How does flying help a cockroach to survive?

    _____

3. Why does the writer say it's a safe bet there will still be cockroaches in the

    future, even after people have gone? _____

    _____

4. Draw a cockroach of the future, from the year 5 000.

    ┌───┐
    │   │
    │   │
    │   │
    │   │
    │   │
    │   │
    │   │
    │   │
    │   │
    │   │
    │   │
    └───┘

Eyes in the Night

When Harry woke up, he didn't know where he was. Everything was strange. Then he remembered—he was at Nanna's house. His family was having a holiday at her house by the sea.

Harry was thirsty. He wanted a glass of water. He was just about to get out of bed when he saw the eyes on the floor!

They were yellow, big and round, with black slits in the middle. They were looking straight at him. They seemed to glow in the moonlight coming through the window.

A monster! It must be a monster! Harry was very scared. He was too scared to call out for Mum or Dad. He pulled the blankets right up to his nose. He watched the monster's eyes. They were coming closer!

The eyes were moving slowly. They rocked gently from side to side, like a — snake! It must be a giant snake. Harry would be eaten up in his own bed! The eyes came closer.

The monster was so close now Harry could hear it. It made a funny, faint sort of *rumbling* sound. Harry opened his mouth to scream—and the monster leaped!

The yellow eyes flew through the air, straight at Harry!

Then Nanna's friendly black cat, Thomas, landed on the bed. It licked Harry's face and purred happily.

Level A

1. Why did Harry want to get out of bed?

   _____

   _____

2. What did Harry think the eyes belonged to?

   _____

3. What colour eyes does Nanna's cat have?

   _____

Level B

1. What do you think happened next?

   _____

   _____

   _____

   _____

2. What really was the *rumbling* sound Harry could hear?

   _____

   _____

3. Why would Thomas the cat be happy?

   _____

   _____

4. Suggest three different things that the 'eyes in the dark' could have seen.

   _____

   _____

   _____

   _____

Level C

1. What might have happened if there really was a monster in the room?

    _____

    _____

2. What would you have done if you were Harry?

    _____

    _____

3. Why did Harry pull the blankets up to his nose?

    _____

    _____

4. Describe a situation where you have been scared.

    _____

    _____

    _____

    _____

    _____

    _____

    _____

    _____

    _____

    _____

    _____

    _____

    _____

    _____

A Real Australian

The Red Kangaroo is a famous Australian animal. It moves by jumping on its long back legs. Its long, heavy tail helps it keep its balance. If chased, a large kangaroo can reach a speed of 40 kilometres an hour. One jump may be eight metres long and up to 3 metres high.

The Red Kangaroo is found mainly in the dry grasslands of Australia. It usually travels in small groups called 'mobs'. Each mob has about 12 kangaroos.

When a baby Red Kangaroo is born, it weighs only 28 grams! After being born, it crawls through the mother's fur to her pouch. In hard times, the mother kangaroo can stop the baby from being born until there is enough grass for her to eat.

The mother feeds the baby (called a 'joey') with milk from her body. The joey will spend at least a year in the pouch.

If a kangaroo is being chased and can not run away, it will turn and fight. It will lean back on its tail and kick with its back legs. These legs are very, very strong and have large claws. The front legs are used to hold, not to box with, as you often see in cartoons.

Kangaroos can live for up to 20 years. A kangaroo never stops growing bigger, so an old kangaroo can be very large indeed. There are probably millions of kangaroos of all types in Australia. They were a very important food for Aborigines.

Level A

1. What helps a kangaroo keep its balance?

    _____

    _____

2. What is a baby kangaroo called?

    _____

3. When does a kangaroo stop growing?

    _____

4. Where in Australia would you find the Red Kangaroo?

    _____

Level B

1. Why does a joey spend so much time in its mother's pouch?

    _____

    _____

2. Can you think of a reason why kangaroos live and travel in 'mobs'?

    _____

    _____

3. If in danger, what is the *first* thing a kangaroo tries to do?

    _____

    _____

4. Suggest a reason for calling a baby kangaroo a 'joey'.

    _____

    _____

    _____

Level C

1. Look at the title of the article. Why has the writer called it this?

    _____

    _____

2. Why won't ordinary farm fences keep a kangaroo out?

    _____

    _____

3. Should animals like kangaroos be protected from hunters? Why?

    _____

    _____

    _____

    _____

4. Complete this table of statistics on the Red Kangaroo.

    Country of origin: _____

    Maximum Speed: _____

    Length of jump: _____

    Height of jump: _____

    Size of group: _____

    Group name: _____

    Weight at birth: _____

    Distinguishing Features:

    _____

    _____

    Distinguishing Habits

    _____

    _____

    _____

The First Pets

The first wild animals tamed by humans were dogs. This happened in Europe about 10 000 years ago.

These first 'dogs' were not like we have now. They may have been small wolves. Or they may have been a breed of dog like the Australian dingo.

These dogs probably came near humans to steal scraps of food. Some of their puppies were 'adopted' by people and grew up with them. These pups were quite tame as they grew up. They thought the humans were part of their 'pack'!

Humans realised the dogs were a help to them in a number of ways. The dogs helped them to hunt. They could smell and hear danger before people could. They helped keep people warm on cold nights. They were *fun* to have!

Over a long time, people were able to breed the dogs for different jobs. Some were for hunting; some for herding; and some just for pets. These dogs looked quite different from each other. For example, a German Shepherd looks a lot different from a Yorkshire terrier!

Now, of course, there are many different types of dogs. Dog breeders think there are more than 400 different breeds. That number keeps increasing with new breeds.

Since those early days, humans and dogs have always been together. Today, dogs depend on humans for their survival more than any other animal.

Level A

1. The Australian dingo is a type of _____ .

2. How many breeds of dogs are there now?

   _____

   _____

3. How long have dogs been 'tamed' by humans?

   _____

4. For what different tasks were dogs bred?

   _____

   _____

Level B

1. How can a dog keep someone warm on a cold night?

   _____

   _____

2. Why does the number of dog breeds keep increasing?

   _____

   _____

3. Explain why most dogs need people to survive.

   _____

   _____

4. Suggest some reasons why dogs live in 'packs' in the wild.

   _____

   _____

   _____

5. What other animals have a 'pack mentality'?

   _____

Level C

1. For what reason do you think people first 'adopted' dogs?

   _____

   _____

2. How could dogs help humans to hunt?

   _____

   _____

3. Why is a German Shepherd so different from a Yorkshire terrier?

   _____

   _____

4. Provide arguments 'for' and 'against' purchasing a dog for your family.

   For

   _____

   _____

   _____

   _____

   _____

   Against

   _____

   _____

   _____

   _____

   _____

   Your conclusion

   _____

   _____

   _____

What a Whopper!

The largest animals ever to have been on the earth are still living today!

Most children think dinosaurs were the biggest, but in fact the Blue Whale is much bigger. How big? Well, one Blue Whale was measured at nearly 34 metres long! It probably weighed more than 220 tonnes!

Everything about the Blue Whale is big! Even its tongue may weigh up to four tonnes! They also call to each other in big voices. They can be heard over 800 kilometres away. They are easily the loudest living creatures.

Does it make you wonder what such a huge animal eats? Blue Whales feed on small fish and 'krill'. Krill are tiny animals like shrimp. A Blue Whale strains them out of the water with a special 'rake' inside its mouth. One whale may eat up to four *tonnes* of krill a day.

Because they are mammals (like humans), Blue Whales breathe air. This means they must come to the surface of the water to breathe. The 'waterspout' a whale blows is not really water at all—it is hot breath and water vapour.

Whales are also warm-blooded. Mothers feed their babies on milk from their bodies. By the time they are a year old, those 'babies' may weigh more than 20 tonnes! They can live up to 45 years.

Whales were once hunted in all the world's seas. So many were killed, they were in danger of becoming extinct. Today, most countries have made laws to stop whales being killed, although some still hunt these gentle giants for food and oil.

Reading and Comprehending

Level A

1. Which is bigger — a dinosaur or a Blue Whale?

   _____

2. Blue Whales eat krill. What is krill?

   _____

   _____

3. How much krill may a whale eat in one day?

   _____

   _____

4. Explain 'waterspout'.

   _____

   _____

   _____

Level B

1. Why does a whale eat so much krill every day?

   _____

   _____

2. Does a whale sleep on the bottom of the ocean? How do you know?

   _____

   _____

3. What would happen if all countries kept on hunting whales?

   _____

   _____

4. Explain the similarities between whales and humans.

   _____

   _____

   _____

Level C

1.   Explain why the article is called 'What a Whopper!'.

      _____

      _____

2.   Why do you think most countries stopped hunting whales?

      _____

      _____

3.   Why do you think the writer calls whales 'gentle giants'?

      _____

      _____

      _____

4.   In the past whales have been killed for their blubber and body parts. This practice still
      continues in some parts of the world. Is this good or bad? Explain your position.

      _____

      _____

      _____

      _____

      _____

      _____

      _____

Wings of Fire

Phil and Jill were two parrots. They lived on an island in the middle of the ocean. It was a very nice island, with palm trees and waterfalls—and no people. Phil and Jill were very happy.

Then, one day, a big ship stopped at the island. Men came ashore from the ship. They had machines that clanked and snorted all day and all night. Phil and Jill were very frightened. They hid in the trees to watch what happened.

First, the men knocked down all the trees in a wide strip down the middle of the island. Then they smoothed the ground. Then they covered it with concrete. Next, they built houses and huts down one side of the concrete strip. Finally, other men painted a white stripe down the middle of the concrete.

Then all the people went away. The island became very quiet again. Slowly, the animals came out of their hiding places. The brave ones even played games on the wide concrete strip. They forgot about the people.

One day, Phil and Jill were flying over the island. Suddenly, a strange black bird flew past them. It was huge! It held its wings out stiffly from its sides and *screamed* as it flew by very fast. Smoke and flame whooshed from its tail.

Phil and Jill were blown all round the sky. When they finally stopped tumbling, they hurried to a nearby tree to watch. They saw the strange bird land on the wide concrete strip.

'He was in a hurry, wasn't he?' Phil said to Jill. 'And did you hear him scream!'

'Yes,' said Jill. 'But you would scream too if *your* tail feathers were on fire!'

Level A

1. Phil and Jill were two

    _____.

2. What colour stripe was painted on the concrete?

    _____

    What was the purpose of this strip?

    _____

3. Why did Phil and Jill hide in the trees?

    _____

    _____

    _____

Level B

1. What was it the men actually built?

    _____

2. If it wasn't really a bird that scared Phil and Jill, what was it?

    _____

    _____

3. Why were Phil and Jill 'blown all round the sky'?

    _____

    _____

    _____

4. What types of animal do you think would have been playing games on the concrete strip?

    _____

    _____

    _____

Level C

1.   What possible reason could people have for an airport on the island?

     _____

     _____

2.   Why did Phil and Jill think the jet was another bird?

     _____

     _____

3.   If you were Phil or Jill, what might you do next?

     _____

     _____

4.   Aeroplanes are a cause of noise pollution, especially near airports. Provide arguments
     'for' and 'against' an airport near your home.

     For

     _____

     _____

     _____

     _____

     _____

     _____

     Against

     _____

     _____

     _____

     _____

     _____

     _____

The Speed Champion

What do you think is the fastest animal in the world? A shark? A cheetah? A human being?

No, the fastest animal in the world is, of course, a bird. The Peregrine is a small falcon that kills its prey by folding its wings and diving on it from a great height.

During this dive, it can reach 240 kilometres an hour—or even faster! (Some people say it can reach **440** kilometres an hour!) It hits its prey in the back of the head with its claws. But you don't have to worry. The Peregrine lives on other birds which it attacks in flight. (It sometimes eats small mammals, reptiles and insects—but not people!)

The Peregrine is not a large bird. The male is only between 35 - 45 cm long and weighs up to 750 grams. The female is slightly larger and heavier. But it attacks (and kills) birds up to the size of a goose—in flight! If the Peregrine hits its target, it usually has its dinner! But, strangely, the Peregrine misses more targets than it hits. It might only get one target out of every ten tries!

The Peregrine is not very fussy about its nest. It usually just makes a scrape in the earth on a cliff ledge. Sometimes, it takes an old nest left behind by another bird. It is found in many parts of the world. It likes to be in open areas, well away from people.

Twenty years ago, the Peregrine was in danger of becoming extinct. Now, its numbers are slowly increasing.

Level A

1. What type of bird is the Peregrine?

   _____

   _____

2. True or false?: The Peregrine is a large bird.

   _____

3. A female Peregrine is larger: smaller: about the same size as a male?

   _____

4. Provide some statistics to illustrate the pergrine's speed.

   _____

   _____

5. How does the peregrine attack its prey?

   _____

   _____

Level B

1. Why does the Peregrine falcon dive so fast?

   _____

   _____

2. Why do you think the Peregrine misses so many targets?

   _____

   _____

3. For what reason might Peregrines like to nest away from people?

   _____

   Why is this becoming more difficult?

   _____

   _____

Level C

1. If the Peregrine couldn't dive on its prey, what might it have to eat?

    _____

    _____

2. Is it fair for the Peregrine to kill other animals? Why?

    _____

    _____

3. What possible reasons might explain why the Peregrine nearly died out?

    _____

    _____

4. Draw a picture of a Peregrine's nest showing as much detail as possible. Include labels.

Boats 'n' Things that Float

There is no way we will ever know what the first 'boat' was — or who 'invented' it. Most likely, it was just a tree trunk that someone held onto and floated across or down a river. From there, it would have been just a short step to building a raft by tying a few logs together. A tree hollowed out by lightning or fire may have been the way people found out you could ride *in* a boat as well as *on* it!

These 'boats' would have only been able to drift with the current or tide. Soon, people wanted a way to make boats go where *they* wanted them to go. At first, they probably just pushed their boats through shallow water with long poles. After that came paddles, and then oars.

But for deep-water travel, something else was needed. Sails were invented—probably not by any one person, but by many people at about the same time in different countries. By now, the floating log 'boat' had grown into the hull shape we know today—pointed at the bow and with a rudder for steering. Ways to keep the boat stable, such as outriggers or heavy keels, were also added to deep-water boats.

For many hundreds of years, large boats were made from one material — timber. Highly-skilled shipbuilders spent years handcrafting the finest wood into ships to explore the world. But shipbuilding with timber was slow and expensive.

Eventually, steel took over as the main building material. There were a number of reasons for this: steel is easier to work with; it is *much* faster to build with; it is far stronger (meaning ships can be larger) and it can be made easily into many shapes. Its biggest weakness — rust — can be kept under control by careful maintenance.

In recent times, people have been able to afford boats simply for relaxation and leisure. This boat can be made from a variety of materials, but fibreglass and aluminium are by far the most popular. It may be a canoe, a simple open runabout, a cabin cruiser, a ski boat, a fishing boat, a yacht, or a millionaire's luxury launch. It can be powered by good old human muscle, the wind, outboard engines, inboard engines or inboard/outboard engines!

Some 'boats', like the sailboard, are about as simple as you can get: one person, the wind on a sail, the sea and a board that floats. Some, like the experimental boats that actually 'fly' *above* the waves and need computers to help control them, are about as complicated as you can get. But somewhere — way, way back in time — they all owe their existence to those people who realised that something which floated could *carry* something (or someone) else.

Level A

1.   What is said to be the biggest weakness of steel for building ships?

     _____

2.   What was needed for deep-water travel?

     _____

     _____

3.   Before steel, what were most boats made from?

     _____

     _____

4.   _____ and _____ are the two most popular building materials for 'leisure' boats.

Level B

1.   Place these means of propelling a boat in sequence from first discovered to last discovered: sails; outboard engines; oars; drifting; poles

     _____

2.   In the very first paragraph, explain why the word 'boat' is in quotation marks.

     _____

     _____

3.   Explain why sails were so important.

     _____

     _____

4.   Explain why a boat is pointed at the bow.

     _____

5.   Describe some different boats used for leisure activities.

     _____

Level C

1.   Why don't we know who invented the boat?

     _____

     _____

2.   What might have been one *advantage* of building ships with timber?

     _____

     _____

3.   List three advantages and three disadvantages of using engines in boats.

     _____   _____

     _____   _____

     _____   _____

4.   In two paragraphs, write what you think a boat of the year 2100 will be like.
     (Describe what it will look like, what it will be made from, what it will be used for, how
     fast it will go, what will power it and so on.)

     _____

     _____

     _____

     _____

     _____

     _____

     _____

     _____

     _____

     _____

     _____

A Tall Tale!

Jodie put her hand up as soon as her teacher asked who had any news.

'Me! Me! Pick me!' she said, unable to hide her excitement.

Very well, Jodie,' said her teacher. 'You may go first.'

Jodie stood out the front of the class.

'Good morning everybody,' she started. 'Well, on the weekend, I went fishing with my grandad. And we went in his boat. And when we were fishing, my grandad told me we were anchored at the very same place where he had lost his wedding ring over the side 20 years before. It had fallen in the sea and he never saw it again. He said Nanna was very cross because she gave him the wedding ring.'

'My goodness,' said Jodie's teacher. 'I'll bet your Nanna was upset about that!'

'Yes, she was,' said Jodie. 'But ten minutes after Grandad told me that story, he started to sneeze. And he sneezed so hard that his false teeth shot out of his mouth and went over the side of the boat. They sank before Grandad could get the net. For a minute, I thought Grandad was going to jump over after them. Then I thought he might throw *me* overboard to get them! I really expected him to pack up and head for shore after that. But because we were already out at sea, he decided we would keep on fishing.

'What made it worse was that we only caught one fish the whole day — and I caught it, not Grandad. So he wasn't in a very happy mood. When we got home and told Nanna what had happened, she wasn't in a very happy mood either.

'Then I went with Grandad into the backgarden to clean the fish. And while he was cleaning it, guess what he found inside?'

'Wait a minute,' said Jodie's teacher. 'You're not going to tell us he found his false teeth inside the fish, are you? Because I don't think I could believe that!'

Level A

1. When did Jodie and her grandad go fishing?

    _____

    _____

2. Why was Jodie's Grandma so cross 20 years ago?

    _____

    _____

3. What happened when Jodie's grandad sneezed?

    _____

    _____

4. What did they find when they were cleaning the fish?

    _____

Level B

1. Give two reasons why Grandad was not in a happy mood.

    _____

    _____

2. Why would her grandad's voice sound funny when he talked?

    _____

    _____

3. Do you think Jodie was telling a true story? Explain your answer.

    _____

    _____

4. Why do writers give their stories names?

    _____

    _____

    _____

Level C

1. What is a tall story?

   _____

   _____

2. Do you think this is a good tall story? Why?

   _____

   _____

3. Why do you think Jodie's teacher interrupted her?

   _____

   _____

4. Write a plan for your own 'tall story'.

   Beginning

   _____

   _____

   _____

   _____

   Development

   _____

   _____

   _____

   _____

   Conclusion

   _____

   _____

   _____

   _____

Danger! Beware!

There are many animals (and plants) in the oceans and seas that are poisonous. They may inject a poison into their victim, or their flesh may poison us if we eat it.

Jellyfish

The most 'famous' poisonous jellyfish is the sea wasp. This pale jellyfish with its long trailing tentacles can even kill humans. It is lucky for us that these jellyfish are found in only one place—off the northern and north-east coasts of Australia.

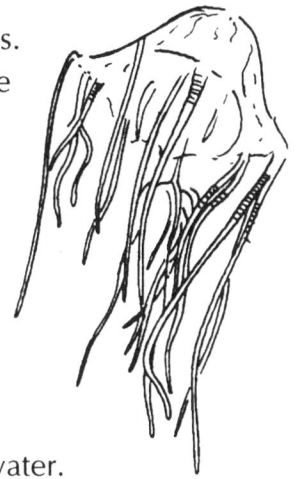

Normally, a jellyfish sting is not that serious. If you are stung, get out of the water. Don't use your hands to brush stings off your skin. Use a towel, sand, clothing or even a stick. Soothing creams or sprays can then be used. If the sting is really bad, get to a doctor as soon as possible.

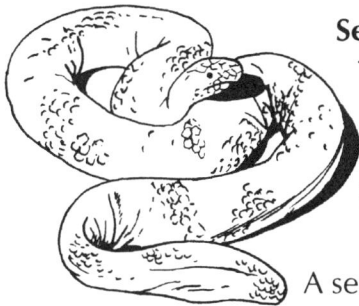

Sea snakes

The chances of being bitten by a sea snake are pretty small. Generally, most sea snakes would rather swim away than bite you. Most people are bitten because they accidentally stepped on the snake or trapped it so it felt threatened.

A sea snake usually has quite small fangs. But its poison is just as deadly as any land snake! If anyone is bitten by a sea snake, wrap a broad, compression bandage over the bitten limb (arms and legs are most often bitten). Keep the patient calm and still and get medical help urgently!

Stonefish

The stonefish is an ugly looking creature usually found hiding in tide pools and among reefs. It belongs to the Scorpionfish family. Because of its shape and colouring (its camouflage), it is extremely hard to see. If it is stood on or picked up, it can inject its poison through up to 18 spines. The pain from the sting can be so extreme it can make the victim unconscious. In many cases, the poison from a stonefish sting can be fatal!

There is a special antidote for stonefish stings. It was developed in Australia. *Immediate* medical help is required for anyone stung by a stonefish.

Stingrays

Stingrays are found in just about any of the world's oceans, where the water is not too cold. They are generally burrowed into the mud or sand, well hidden on the ocean floor. A stingray's sting is in its tail, which it can whip round with deadly force. Although the poison is rarely fatal—it is going to cause a lot of pain to anyone who is stung!

Level A

1. Are jellyfish, sea snakes and stingrays poisonous to eat, or do they inject their poison?

    _____

    _____

2. Why shouldn't you brush stings off with your hands?

    _____

    _____

3. Why are stonefish so hard to see?

    _____

    _____

4. To which fish family does the stonefish belong?

    _____

Level B

1. Are sea wasps, sea snakes, stonefish and stingrays all found in Australia?

    _____

2. What is an 'antidote'?

    _____

3. Name two places in the world where you would NOT find stingrays.

    _____

    _____

4. Why does an angler have to be careful if a stingray is caught?

    _____

    _____

5. Why does the sea snake have difficulty biting humans?

    _____

    _____

Level C

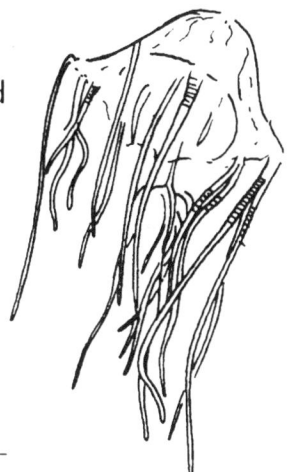

1. Why do you think the antidote to the stonefish poison was developed in Australia?

   _____

   _____

2. When you walk in rock pools, how can you protect yourself from being stung?

   _____

   _____

   _____

3. In most of northern Australia, it is only safe to swim in the sea during the 'Dry' season (from May until October). Why do you think this is?

   _____

   _____

   _____

4. Your friend has just been bitten on the arm by a sea snake. Write what you would do.

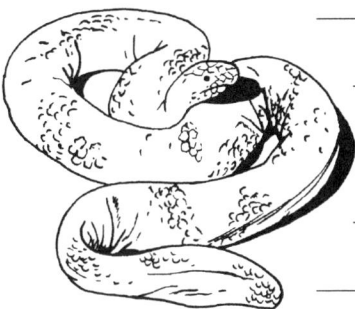

   _____

   _____

   _____

   _____

   _____

   _____

   _____

   _____

   _____

Fishing: For and Against

Fishing is probably the world's most popular sport. Millions and millions of people spend billions and billions each year on tackle, bait, boats, fuel, repairs, four-wheel-drives — just so they can go fishing.

The case for fishing

Of all those millions of people, most of them are after fish to eat. Generally, they are happy with a few fish to feed themselves and their families. They catch fish that are found in huge numbers, so there is little danger of them being fished out.

People can't catch fish every day of the year, either. There are times when the weather is too bad for fishing, times when people may have to go to work, even times when the fish may not be there! These breaks in fishing give the fish a chance to build up their numbers.

Anglers make a huge contribution to the economy. Not only do they spend money directly —as was mentioned earlier — they also spend it indirectly, such as in tax on their equipment or fuel, or in accommodation and airfares. This money keeps many people in work and provides many new jobs each year.

It is also a way of reducing stress. Many people who are stressed turn to drugs or alcohol to help them cope. Fishing, like other recreations, can be both fun and relaxing. People who are relaxed are generally healthier — and much nicer to be near (except for the smell of the bait!).

The case against fishing

There are too many people fishing. The fish aren't farmed or conserved; they are just taken until there is none left. No animal can stand that sort of pressure. Modern cars and boats mean people can now fish even in remote areas of the world—no place is 'safe' for fish.

Too many anglers are greedy. They take more fish than they can possibly use. These often end up just being wasted. They take males and females so that few fish are left to breed, and the numbers fall even further.

Fishing is a blood sport. This means that an animal must die so that a human can have 'fun'. (This applies more to sportsfishing than to fishing for food; at least if a fish is eaten, there is some purpose to it being caught.) Once hooked, fish have little or no chance of escape.

Whatever side you are on — for or against — fishing is an activity that will come under much closer examination in the future.

Level A

1. What is the main reason people catch fish?

_____

_____

2. How do people who fish help the economy?

_____

_____

_____

3. What is a 'blood sport'?

_____

_____

4. What will happen if too many people take too many fish?

_____

_____

Level B

1. Why is fishing such a widely available sport all round the world?

_____

_____

2. What should people do with any extra fish they can't eat?

_____

3. Why would people just throw the fish in the rubbish bin?

_____

_____

4. Can you think of any place in the world where people could not fish?

_____

_____

Level C

1.   Is fishing really a 'sport'? Explain your answer.

_____

_____

2.   Why do anglers often use four-wheel-drive vehicles?

_____

_____

3.   Why do you think fishing might reduce stress?

_____

_____

4.   Choose either 'for' fishing or 'against' fishing. Write your own case, presenting some new ideas.

_____

_____

_____

_____

_____

_____

_____

_____

_____

_____

_____

_____

_____

_____

_____

Green Is Not a Funny Colour

The French have a nice-sounding name for it — *mal de mer*. Our name is less fancy — seasick. Whatever you call it, being seasick is one of the most awful experiences you can have. You won't die from it — but a lot of people feel so sick they wish they could die!

If you are one of those lucky people who doesn't get seasick, have a little sympathy for those who do. What do they feel? Well, firstly, you feel sick in your stomach — and quite often you are sick! You feel dizzy, and as if your arms and legs don't belong to you. Your head feels funny, too, as if there is a steel band right around it — and someone is slowly but steadily tightening that band! Sweat just pours off you and you ache all over. It is NOT nice!

What causes seasickness? Most people believe it is caused by their stomach, so they try not to eat or even think about food. You've probably heard some of the cures involving food — drink lots of water, eat dry bread, don't eat anything fatty, and so on. In truth, none of these will help! The reason is that an upset stomach is only a symptom of seasickness. Because seasickness is caused, believe it or not, by your ears.

The constant movement of a boat upsets the part of your ears that looks after your balance. What happens then is the sort of sick feeling you get if you spin on the spot for too long — only worse! (You can also get a similar movement in cars and planes — which is why seasickness is sometimes called 'motion sickness'.)

What can you do? Well, keeping your head up may help. Lying down may help — but be warned, it may make it much worse! Looking at an object that is not moving, such as the coastline, may help too. There are also medicines you can buy to take before you go on the water. One new idea is a small patch that you stick behind your ear. It slowly releases seasickness medicine into your bloodstream and works for a couple of days.

But for most of us — well, we'll just have to learn to live with seasickness. Or stay on something that doesn't move beneath us!

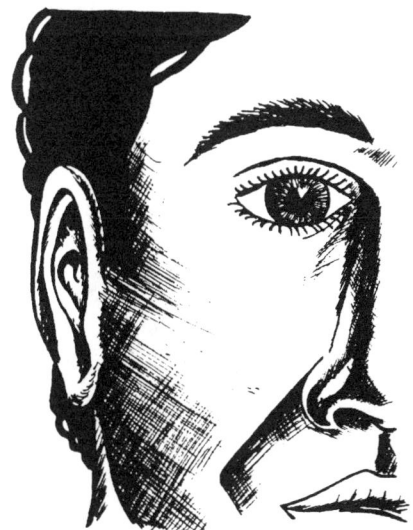

Level A

1. What does *mal de mer* mean?

    _____

2. Seasickness is not caused by your stomach, it is caused by your _____

3. How long do the effects of a seasickness patch last?

    _____

4. Why does a patch last so long?

    _____

    _____

5. What is another name for sea sickness and where can it occur?

    _____

    _____

Level B

1. Why do people think that what they drink or eat will affect their seasickness?

    _____

    _____

2. What is the advantage of using a patch instead of taking seasickness tablets?

    _____

    _____

3. Apart from tablets and patches, what else does the writer suggest might help?

    _____

    _____

4. What sea and weather conditions do you think might make seasickness worse?

    _____

    _____

Level C

1. The writer seems very sympathetic towards people who get seasick. Why do you think this might be?

    _____

    _____

2. Explain the difference between motion sickness and seasickness.

    _____

    _____

    _____

3. Why do seasick people recover so quickly once they are on firm ground?

    _____

    _____

4. If you have been motion sick, write a paragraph describing how you felt.

    If not, explain how you would help a friend who had sea sickness.

    _____

    _____

    _____

    _____

    _____

    _____

    _____

    _____

Shark!

'Don't go water skiing in the bay,' said Uncle Pete.
'There could be sharks in there.'

'Nonsense,' said Kevin, who thought he knew everything.

'I wouldn't go skiing in the bay,' said the man in the petrol station. 'They saw sharks in there last week.'

'Won't hurt me,' said Kevin, smiling.

'You're not going skiing in the bay, are you?' asked the man next to us at the launching ramp. 'I'm sure we saw a shark on our way back a few minutes ago.'

'Rubbish,' said Kevin. 'Anyway, sharks don't worry me!'

Kevin and his two friends Trevor and Leo launched Kevin's shiny new ski boat. Kevin drove away from the ramp very fast, spraying everyone with water. His engine roared as he gunned the boat out into the middle of the bay. The water wasn't any calmer there, it was just that more people could see him there! If there was one thing Kevin liked to do, it was show-off in front of a crowd.

'You drive,' he told Trevor. 'And you can be the observer,' he said to Leo. 'I'm going skiing.'

'What about the sharks?' asked Trevor.

'Forget all about them,' said Kevin. 'You don't have to be scared of sharks.'

He slipped over the back of the boat into the water. He lifted his leg and fitted his ski. Trevor pulled the boat away slowly until the ski rope stretched out tight. Trevor watched forwards while Leo turned his seat round to face backwards. They were ready.

Kevin felt something brush against his leg. Something very large and very hard! Then, not two metres away, a glistening brown fin broke the surface of the water.

Later, when they stopped laughing, both Leo and Trevor said Kevin walked across the top of the water on his way back into the boat! His legs didn't stop churning until he was safely on board, wrapped in a towel. He even left his ski and the ski rope behind.

Leo was bringing in the ski rope hand over hand when the brown fin appeared again.

'There it is!' shouted Kevin. 'Shark! Shark!'

And the dolphin came to the surface, took a deep breath, smiled at Kevin, and dived again.

Level A

1. Why did Kevin go out into the middle of the bay to ski? _____

    _____

2. Who owned the ski boat? _____

3. Who had to pull in the ski rope? _____

4. Which three people warned Kevin not to ski in the bay?

    _____

    _____

    _____

Level B

1. Leo was the 'observer' on the boat. What did he have to do? _____

    _____

    _____

2. Why were Trevor and Leo laughing? _____

    _____

    _____

3. Do you think Kevin had ever seen many sharks? Explain your answer. _____

    _____

    _____

4. Were they skiing in the river or the sea? How do you know? _____

    _____

5. Explain what the author meant by 'walked across the top of the water'. Is this a good
    description?

    _____

    _____

    _____

Level C

1. How do you think Kevin felt about his new ski boat? _____

_____

2. Kevin wasn't very considerate about other people. How do you know this?

_____

_____

3. What do you think Kevin might have learnt from this experience?

_____

_____

_____

4. What do you think might happen the next day, when Leo and Trevor ask Kevin about going skiing again? Write down what you think Kevin would say.

_____

_____

_____

_____

_____

_____

5. Explain a time or incident in your life where you could have been 'more responsible'.

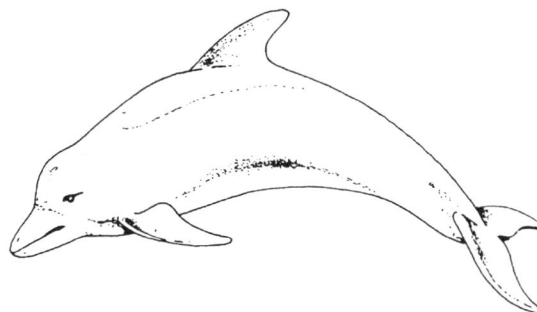

_____

_____

_____

_____

How About the Future?

In many ways (such as fishing), the oceans are already in danger of being overused. We are also polluting our waterways to the point of extreme danger! There is no doubt that, as the population of the earth grows, we will have to look after our seas and oceans better, and keep them cleaner — and, strangely enough, use them even more!

Fish farms

If we keep on taking fish out of the ocean in greater and greater numbers, we will eventually run out of fish. And in the future, as our population increases, fish are going to be an increasingly important food source. Somehow, we must learn to 'farm' fish for food, the same way we now do with sheep or cattle. But the problems are enormous. Fish will have to be bred in HUGE numbers, looked after and fed, until they are ready to be 'harvested'. Just now, we don't know how to do that, except in small experimental farms.

Underwater cities

For many years, films have shown people living under the oceans, usually in cities beneath huge glass domes. There is no doubt that the earth is running out of room. And dry land only makes up 30% of the earth's surface; the remainder is water. So, we may have to go underwater to live in the future.

There will be huge problems with that, as you can imagine. It is possible though, and everything these underwater-people needed could be drawn from the water around them. Their food, air, power, everything, could come from the sea. Can you imagine spending your whole life under water, never feeling sunlight or fresh air? Would you ever be able to come back to the surface?

Super submarines

As computers become more and more 'intelligent', computer-controlled submarines could be sent deep beneath the oceans to carry goods around the world without a single human in the crew. These submarines would be 'cheap' to build, because they would need no lighting, no heating, no air and could operate with pressures that would kill a human. They would probably have a nuclear engine, because this lasts for years without needing to be 'refuelled'.

Each submarine would have its own 'path' to travel. There could be no collisions, because no two submarines would have the same 'path'. But, just suppose there was an accident deep underwater. Can you imagine the damage that could be caused by a leaking nuclear reactor? Or suppose one of these giant submarines is full of oil. If it breaks up on the ocean bottom, we stand no chance of getting to it to pump the cargo into tanks. It would all leak into the oceans. Do we dare take the risk?

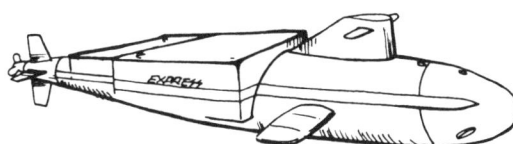

Level A

1. What could super submarines be used for?

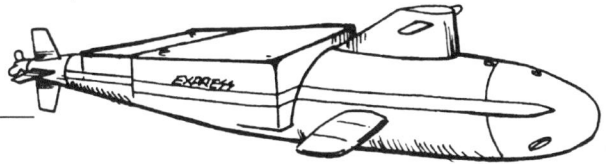

   _____

   _____

   _____

2. What would be the main reason for building cities beneath the sea?

   _____

   _____

3. From where would people in underwater cities get their food and air?

   _____

4. Why might it be necessary to develop fish farms?

   _____

   _____

Level B

1. Why will submarines be so much cheaper if they don't need a crew?

   _____

   _____

2. Name three differences between super submarines and those we have today.

   _____

   _____

3. What percentage of the earth is covered by water? _____

4. How will the super submarines be kept on the right 'path' underneath the seas?

   _____

   _____

5. Do you think all fish species would be suitable for fish farming? Explain!

   _____

Level C

1. In paragraph 2, why has the writer put the word 'harvested' in inverted commas?

    _____

    _____

2. Why is the sea becoming polluted to dangerous levels? _____

    _____

    _____

3. Writers usually have a point of view and a reason for writing an article. Do you think the writer is frightened and worried, or confident problems will be solved? Explain.

    _____

    _____

    _____

    _____

4. Imagine you live in a city under a huge glass dome beneath the sea. Make a list of the advantages and disadvantages of living down there.

    _____

    _____

    _____

    _____

5. What similarities may exist between fish farming and farming on the land?

    _____

    _____

    _____

    _____

    _____

    _____

What's for Dinner?

Finbar was a sea monster. He lived with his mother, Finetta, and his father, Finelder, many, many, *many* metres under the sea. In fact, it was so dark where they lived, they had to carry their own little lights with them on the tip of their nose so they could see.

Not that there was much to see. That far under the sea, it was pretty dull and colourless. In fact, there was mud, mud, and—just to be different—more mud. Their food was pretty boring, too—fish, fish and more fish.

Finbar was bored to tears. He was sick of his life. He wanted some fun! He wanted to see light and colour! He wanted to feel the warmth of the sun on his back! But most of all, he wanted some decent food!

His mother, who loved him very much even if he was as ugly as a poison toad, looked high and low for some different food. At last, she found the wreck of a ship that had sunk. There were no people inside, but there were thousands and thousands of cans of cat food! Oh, she thought, Finbar will be so happy.

And so he was. At every meal, he would crack a hundred cans between his huge jaws and suck out the sweet meat inside. At first, he loved the new food. But after a year, he grew tired of it. After two years, he grew bored with it. And after three years, he positively hated it!

Finally, he told his mother he wanted something else to eat besides fish and cat food. His mother, who loved him very much even if he was as ugly as a poison toad, looked high and low for some different food. One day, she came across a submarine travelling slowly through the deep water. Oh, she thought, Finbar will be so happy.

She brought her son to see the submarine, which was only half his monstrous size.

'Look what I found for you,' she said proudly.

'What on earth is it?' asked Finbar.

'It's a sort of boat thing ... made of metal ... and filled with yummy, juicy people,' his mother explained.

'Oh, no,' moaned Finbar. 'Not more canned food!'

Level A

1. Why did Finbar and his family carry their own little lights with them?

   _____

   _____

2. What was Finbar's main food before his mother found the wrecked ship?

   _____

   _____

3. What are first names of Finbar's mother and father?

   _____ and _____

4. True or false?

   Finbar was about half the size of the submarine. _____

   -

Level B

1. Why was it 'pretty dull and colourless' where the monsters lived?

   _____

   _____

2. What tells you Finbar had very powerful jaws?

   _____

   _____

3. What did Finbar and his family think of people?

   _____

   _____

4. Why did Finetta still love Finbar, even if he was 'as ugly as a poison toad'?

   _____

   _____

   _____

Level C

1. Do you think Finbar would eat the people in the submarine? Explain your answer.

   _____

   _____

2. Suggest three things that Finbar could do to help him get over his boredom.

   _____

   _____

3. Why does the writer not tell you exactly what the monsters look like?

   _____

   _____

4. You are the captain of the submarine. You see Finbar and his mother on an underwater television camera. In a paragraph or two, describe the monsters.

   _____

   _____

   _____

   _____

   _____

   _____

   _____

   _____

   _____

   _____

Atlantis—Lost or Found?

Somewhere in the world is said to be the remains of the fabulous lost continent of Atlantis. According to legend, Atlantis existed about 50 000 years ago, in the *Atlantic* Ocean, somewhere 'beyond the Pillars of Hercules'. The people of Atlantis (the Atlanteans) were supposed to be very advanced in science and engineering—even more advanced than we are today. They were said to have found the secret of unlimited energy and power, using 'crystals' to harness their energy.

Gradually, the stories about Atlanteans grew and grew: they could fly in 'anti-gravity' machines or spaceships; they had weapons like lasers, and talking 'computers'; they could communicate telepathically. When Hollywood got hold of the legend, some films even had the Atlanteans still alive today, living in huge domed cities beneath the sea!

Then, so the original legend goes, something happened, and Atlantis was destroyed, along with all its people. Just what happened, we are not sure. One story is that it was a natural disaster, like an earthquake or volcano (or both together), that sank Atlantis without trace. Another story says that the Atlanteans discovered powers they couldn't control, which eventually broke loose and destroyed them.

At the start of this century, scientists discovered, buried under the earth of Greece, the remains of an entire civilisation, unlike anything they had seen before. They began to think they may have 'discovered' Atlantis. To add to their beliefs, the neighbouring island of Thera seemed to have been responsible for a giant volcanic eruption that destroyed 'Atlantis'.

Despite this 'proof', many people still did not believe Atlantis had been found. Thanks to films, television and writers with terrific imaginations, the favourite spot for finding Atlantis was not Greece but—the Bermuda Triangle! And in 1968, that looked to be coming true, when divers discovered steps, pathways, walls and even 'pyramids' under the water off the coast of Bimini, in the Bermuda Triangle. There was huge excitement! It looked as if Atlantis had finally been discovered. What's more, if Atlantis *was* beneath the Bermuda Triangle, it could help to explain some of the strange things that happened there! Perhaps some of those Atlantean machines, with powers we can't even understand, were still working under the ocean.

But, as usually happens, the next lot of divers to investigate the area said the whole thing was a load of rubbish! All they could find were natural rock formations that looked a *little* bit like walls and roads, but certainly no cities or pyramids or strange machines.

But people still keep looking. Perhaps they are wasting their time, perhaps Atlantis never existed at all. Or maybe they just haven't looked in the right places—like under the snow and ice at the Poles! Maybe it's just that people *need* stories like Atlantis to give them something to imagine—and dream about.

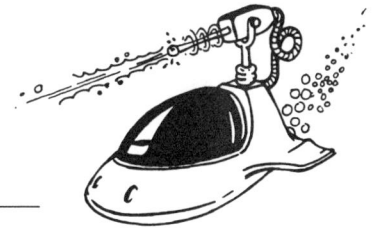

Level A

1.   What were the people of Atlantis called?

_____

2.   According to the original legend, in which ocean was Atlantis to be found?

_____

3.   Why did scientists believe they had discovered Atlantis in Greece?

_____

_____

4.   Where is the favourite spot for finding Atlantis?

_____

_____

Level B

1.   What does the writer mean by saying 'When Hollywood got hold of the legend …'?

_____

_____

2.   Why do you think people believed that divers had found the ruins of cities

beneath the ocean off Bermuda? _____

_____

_____

3.   What happened after the 'discovery' was announced?

_____

_____

4.   If Atlantis was discovered in the Bermuda Triangle, how would that explain some of the weird things that happen there?

_____

_____

Level C

1. Do you think scientists have taken the idea of Atlantis seriously? Explain your answer.

_____

_____

2. Do you think that the writer believes in the existence of Atlantis? Why?

_____

_____

3. In your own words, explain why you think people are still searching for Atlantis.

_____

_____

4. You are a diver who has just found ruins on the ocean floor in the Bermuda Triangle. In a paragraph or two, describe what you are seeing.

_____

_____

_____

_____

_____

_____

_____

_____

_____

_____

_____

_____

_____

A Strange Triangle

Most people have heard of the Bermuda Triangle, but not many know exactly where it is. Have a look at a map of the USA. Draw a line from Miami (Florida) east to Puerto Rico, then north to Bermuda and back to Miami. Now you have, roughly, the Bermuda Triangle.

What makes the Triangle so special? Well, there *seems* to be an awful lot of strange things happening there; things for which we have no natural explanation. And it's not just recently this has been happening either, although the area has received more publicity in the last twenty or so years.

So, just what happens in the Triangle that is so weird? Quite a lot of things! For example, compasses often go crazy, spinning round or even pointing in the wrong direction altogether. Christopher Columbus noticed this 500 years ago! It is still reported by ships and even aircraft today. Luckily, modern navigation doesn't rely on magnetic compasses any more!

There also seems to be something that can affect time in the Triangle. There have been stories of light aircraft, for example, flying into strange fogs. When they came out the other side, after just a few minutes flying time to them, it was to find that they had been gone for several hours! There's also the pilot who got lost. A control tower directed the plane to an airfield on a nearby island. The people on the island could see the plane circling overhead—but the pilot couldn't see them or the buildings or cars or anything! To the pilot, the island was totally deserted—the way it had been *before* the airfield had been built! Eventually, the pilot just flew away, still thinking she was lost.

You can't even trust your eyes in the Bermuda Triangle! Perhaps the most famous case was the flight of five torpedo bombers which took off from Fort Lauderdale in Florida on 5 December 1945. It was just an ordinary training flight—but the planes never returned. Somehow, these very experienced pilots got lost. Their compasses and then their radios stopped working properly—and they kept heading away from safety. The last message from the flight leader said that things looked 'wrong' and 'strange' to them all. No one will ever know what he meant, because the flight just disappeared. And so did a huge aircraft sent up to search for them!

There are many, many cases of missing ships in the Triangle, but the most famous is the *Marie Celeste*. The *Marie Celeste* was found in 1872, floating abandoned in the Triangle, with all sails set. But there was not a single person on board! Even though there was food and water, and the ship was in good condition, the crew had gone, disappeared without taking even their pipes or tobacco. What happened? Was it aliens? A waterspout? People from Atlantis? Did a monster octopus drag them to their deaths? No one will ever be able to say for sure—but some weird things *are* happening in the Bermuda Triangle!

Level A

1. Why do people think the Bermuda Triangle is special?

    _____

    _____

2. Name two of the weird things that might happen in the Triangle.

    _____

    _____

3. Which is the most famous of the missing ships in the Triangle?

    _____

4. In the story about the pilot who became lost, was the pilot male or female?

    _____

Level B

1. What might happen in a sailing boat if the compass didn't work properly?

    _____

    _____

2. Why do you think the Bermuda Triangle has received more publicity

    in the last 20 years or so? _____

    _____

3. Why didn't the Fort Lauderdale torpedo bombers just turn around and

    head back to safety? _____

    _____

    _____

4. What tells you the *Marie Celeste*'s crew left in a hurry?

    _____

    _____

Level C

1. Do you think the writer believes there is something funny about the Bermuda Triangle? Why?

    _____

    _____

    _____

2. What *facts* does the writer present to support the claims in the article?

    _____

    _____

3. What do you think is the most likely reason the crew disappeared from the *Marie Celeste*? What do you think is the *least* likely reason?

    _____

    _____

    _____

    _____

4. You are the flight leader in the flight of aircraft from Fort Lauderdale. In a paragraph or two, describe what you are seeing that is 'wrong' and 'strange'.

    _____

    _____

    _____

    _____

    _____

    _____

    _____

    _____

    _____

    _____

Batteries Included

There was *definitely* something strange about Melissa's new teacher, Miss Matthews. But when Melissa spoke to her friends about it, they thought she was imagining things.

'Don't be silly,' said her best friend in the world, Samantha. 'She's just the same as any other person.'

'Weird?' said Kylie. 'Lissie, *all* teachers are weird; this one's no different!'

'Nonsense, dear,' said her mum, when Melissa told her. 'I'm sure you're just imagining it. Once you get used to Miss Matthews, you'll find she is just like everyone else.'

'She'd have to be weird to teach you, anyway,' said Melissa's younger sister, Jessica.

'Not half as weird as after teaching *you* for a week, squirt-features,' Melissa replied sweetly.

'That's enough out of you two,' said their dad from behind his newspaper. He'd heard it all before. 'Set the table and stop arguing.'

But later that night in bed, just before she fell asleep, Melissa decided that she was right after all— there *was* something weird about Miss Matthews. And she was going to find out what it was!

The following day, she put her plan into action. It wasn't much of a plan, really. All she could think of was to follow Miss Matthews for the whole day at school, and try not to let her out of her sight.

At morning play, Miss Matthews went into the staffroom and just sat at one of the tables. She didn't have a cup of tea or a biscuit. None of the other teachers spoke to her, either, which Melissa thought was rude.
Miss Matthews did the same thing at lunchtime, until Mrs Hoi-Poi, the head teacher, whispered something in her ear. Then Miss Matthews stood up and went out and did playground duty.

But at afternoon play, Miss Matthews did something different. Instead of going into the staffroom, she went into the office. She knocked on Mrs Hoi-Poi's door and stood and waited until it was opened. She went inside the room and the door closed behind her.

Melissa raced around the office block and scooted up the branches of a small apple tree. From there she could see straight in the office windows, without being seen herself. It was against school rules to climb the trees, but just then Melissa couldn't have cared less. When she saw what was happening, she nearly fell out of the tree with surprise anyway!

Mrs Hoi-Poi had a long electrical cord in one hand. One end was plugged into a wall socket. With her free hand, she reached out and swept up Miss Matthews' hair. Miss Matthews just stood there, not moving.

Then Mrs Hoi-Poi plugged the power cord into the socket in the back of Miss Matthews' neck.

Level A

1. What was Melissa's nickname?How do you know?

    _____

    _____

    _____

2. How many children were there in Melissa's family?

    _____

3. What job did Mrs Hoi-Poi have in the school?

    _____

4. What was the first weird thing Melissa noticed when she started

    watching Miss Matthews? _____

    _____

Level B

1. What do you think Miss Matthews was? What tells you this?

    _____

    _____

2. For what reason do you think Melissa calls Jessica 'squirt-features'?

    _____

    _____

3. Do you think Melissa and Jessica said these types of things to each other often?

    What tells you this? _____

    _____

    _____

4. Were the other teachers being rude in not talking to Miss Matthews in the
    staffroom? Why? _____

    _____

Level C

1. What would be the advantages of having Miss Matthews for a teacher?

    What would be the disadvantages? _____

    _____

    _____

2. What do you think Mrs Hoi-Poi whispered in Miss Matthews' ear?

    _____

    _____

3. Discuss the title of the story. Find another title of your own.

    _____

    _____

4. In a paragraph, describe to the rest of the class what Melissa has just seen.

    _____

    _____

    _____

    _____

    _____

    _____

    _____

    _____

    _____

    _____

    _____

    _____

    _____

    _____

'I Want to Drink Your Blood…'

It is 1732 in Yugoslavia. You are a soldier, one of twenty-four sent from Belgrade with other government officials and officers to investigate a report of a vampire in a small country town. The sun is just beginning to set as you march to the grave where the suspected vampire lies. The headstone shows that the person in the grave, a man, died three years ago. Yet, in the past few weeks, he is supposed to have killed five of his nieces and nephews, sucking them dry of their blood. You begin to dig.

Finally, the coffin is opened. Inside is the man. You cannot believe your eyes. He looks to be perfectly healthy, as if he is just asleep. An officer bravely places his hand on the 'vampire's' chest—and cries out when he detects a heartbeat!

Immediately, he orders a steel bar to be hammered through the vampire's chest and into his heart. As the bar pierces the heart, fresh red blood, mixed with a white fluid, spurts out. The body is buried again, in lime this time, and there are no more reports of vampires from that village.

Sound like a good fairy story? A script for a film? Well, it's neither of those. It's actually recorded in history as a *true story*. But does that mean vampires are true; that they actually exist?

No, not really. But during that time in Europe, people believed absolutely and utterly that there were such things as vampires. And if you believe in something that strongly, your mind can twist things to make them appear to be the way you expect them to be. Where did the stories about vampires come from then? No one knows for sure, but there are a few ideas about it.

Back then, it wasn't unusual for people to be buried in special 'tombs' called mausoleums. Often, they were buried with treasures and offerings of food and wine. Starving beggars would break into these mausoleums at night to steal what they could and, because it was usually dry inside, to sleep out of the rain. If anyone saw one of these people in the moonlight—or even worse, saw one 'wake up' from the dead—you can imagine their fear, and the story they would later tell!

Another reason for a belief in vampires could be plain, simple ignorance. 'Doctors' during these times knew nothing about trances or comas; even as late as the mid-1800s there was still confusion among doctors as to how you could tell when someone was 'really' dead. Up until recent times, it is probably true to say that literally thousands and thousands of people were buried alive! Imagine coming out of a coma to find yourself being buried in a coffin! Or, just as bad, imagine yourself in the position of an undertaker, when the 'corpse' suddenly sits up and 'comes back to life'!

Very few people today still believe in vampires; such creatures just have no foundation in truth. But there is one funny thing, though. Have you ever noticed how, after your teacher has been giving you a hard time and making you work like a slave all day, you feel very tired—sort of … *drained?* Makes you stop and think about teachers, doesn't it!

Level A

1. How long had the 'dead' man been in the coffin?

    _____

2. Why did the officer 'cry out'?

    _____

    _____

3. Does this article tell you that vampires were real? Explain your answer.

    _____

    _____

4. Give two reasons why the stories about vampires might have started.

    _____

    _____

Level B

1. In your own words, what is this article trying to tell you?

    _____

    _____

    _____

    _____

2. Why do you think people would be buried with treasures and food and wine?

    _____

    _____

3. How do you 'kill' a vampire? _____

    _____

4. Why were people in earlier times more likely to believe in vampires than we are today?

    _____

    _____

Level C

1. Which do you think would be worse: 'waking up' to find yourself buried alive; or being an undertaker and suddenly having one of the 'corpses' sit up? Why?

    _____

    _____

    _____

    _____

2. Why do you think the writer places the word 'Doctors' in quotation marks when speaking about the 1700s?

    _____

    _____

    _____

3. How well does the writer explain what vampires really were? Why?

    _____

    _____

4. Using your imagination, write an explanation for what *werewolves* might have really been.

    _____

    _____

    _____

    _____

    _____

    _____

    _____

    _____

    _____

    _____

    _____

They Just Disappeared

What happened to the dinosaurs? About 65 000 000 years ago, these creatures, which had ruled the earth for many millions of years, suddenly 'died out'. Why? How?

One explanation is that it simply grew too cold for them. Apparently, about the time the dinosaurs began to die out, there *was* a general 'cooling down' of the earth. And how did that happen?

Well, the most popular theory is that the earth was hit by a *very* large meteorite. The impact created an explosion which threw a huge cloud of debris (dust, dirt etc.) into the upper atmosphere, where it drifted around for a long time. This cloud was so thick, it partially blocked the sun's rays—and so the earth cooled down a little. Unable to adapt to such a rapid temperature change, the dinosaurs died out. This theory is given support by the fact that many other creatures—both on land and in the sea—died out at about the same time, which is what *would* happen in the event of such a large catastrophe.

One immediate argument against this theory is that no crater large enough has ever been found. But what if the meteorite landed in the sea, or on a part of the earth that is now under the sea? There are many areas beneath the sea that have not yet been explored, and probably won't be in our lifetime!

Thanks to television, films and books, you'll hear many other 'stories' about what caused the dinosaurs to become extinct. But, not so strangely, you won't find many facts presented to back these theories up!

One popular story is that the dinosaurs were destroyed by aliens who wanted to populate the planet with their own creatures—humans! According to this theory, the dinosaurs were too much of a threat, and so they were wiped out. If *any* evidence is found to support this theory, it will cause an absolute sensation! But so far, as you might guess, nothing has been found!

Another theory is that the earth's vegetation changed quickly, and the dinosaurs were 'poisoned' when they ate this vegetation, or when they killed and ate prey that had been feeding on the vegetation. Unfortunately for the people who believe in this theory, scientists now know that new species of dinosaurs were evolving all the time, right up until they died out—including many herbivores that were able to eat and thrive on the 'new' vegetation!

What it all boils down to is that, like most mysteries, no one really knows the answer for sure. You might even be wondering what all the fuss is about when it happened so many millions of years ago. Well, think about this. The dinosaurs 'ruled the earth' for many millions of years, and yet they died out almost 'overnight' (in geological terms). Humans have only been around for a bit less than 4 000 000 years. How long will we last?

Level A

1.   About how long is it since dinosaurs have been on the earth?

     _____

2.   True or false: Dinosaurs were a threat to early humans. (Explain your answer.)

     _____

     _____

3.   Give the most likely reason why the dinosaurs died out.

     _____

     _____

4.   If a giant meteorite did hit the earth in the past, why haven't we found the crater?

     _____

     _____

Level B

1.   Does the writer believe that aliens wiped out the dinosaurs?

     Explain your answer. _____

     _____

2.   Why would any evidence that aliens destroyed the dinosaurs and put humans on the earth cause 'an absolute sensation!'?

     _____

     _____

3.   Which is the most likely theory to explain how the dinosaurs died out?

     _____

     _____

4.   Why does it make any difference how the dinosaurs died out?

     _____

     _____

Level C

1. Why do you think there are so many theories about what happened to the dinosaurs?

    _____

    _____

2. You have just gone back in time and come face to face with a dinosaur. Describe how you feel.

    _____

    _____

    _____

    _____

3. Considering humans weren't even around then, why do think people today are so fascinated by dinosaurs?

    _____

    _____

    _____

    _____

4. In your own words, in a paragraph or two, describe another theory explaining how the dinosaurs died out.

    _____

    _____

    _____

    _____

    _____

    _____

    _____

    _____

    _____

Premonition

Julia was frightened—and tired. She'd had the same dream every night now for a week. Each night, it had woken her up, crying. And each time she had been too afraid to go back to sleep, so she had just lain in bed until the sun rose and the world came back to life. She hadn't told her parents about the dream. They would be worried about her, and she didn't want to spoil their holiday; she knew how much they had looked forward to it. She was lucky they had been letting her sleep in her own hotel room, or they surely would have heard her crying in the night.

It wasn't even as if she could make any sense of the dream. In it, a giant arrowhead came plunging from the sky. Revolving gracefully, falling in slow motion, it headed straight for her. Julia couldn't tell what it was—but she knew if it hit her she was dead. In this dream, she was sitting down. She felt she should get up and run, but something was stopping her. In desperation, Julia looked at her waist. A thick rope was tied around it, knotted in front, holding her in place. Desperately, she tore at the rope until her fingernails bent back and broke.

But she couldn't get the knot undone.

The arrowhead loomed larger and larger, filling her vision, blocking out the sun, until …

She would wake up crying.

'Are you OK, dear?' her mother asked from the front seat of the car. 'I've been speaking to you for the last minute or two, and I'm sure you haven't heard a word I've said.'

'Sorry, Mum. I was a million miles away. What did you say?'

'I was just telling you that we're almost at Potter's Peak. We'll stay the night in the new hotel there. It's called 'The Pyramid'. According to the guide book, it has a lot of facilities for guests, including tennis courts, in-house films, a sauna and swimming pool'

'Sounds great, Mum.' All Julia really wanted to do was lie down and try to get some sleep.

The hotel *was* very modern. Dad eased the car to a stop in front of the reception. Above them, a model of an Egyptian pyramid with the hotel's name on it rotated slowly on a metal pole. Something about it stabbed Julia's heart with an icy knife. She reached for her seatbelt, but the buckle jammed and she couldn't shift it.

'Dad! Dad!' she screamed, suddenly understanding. 'Move the car! Quickly! Move the car!'

Her father, startled, jerked the accelerator and the car, still in gear, shot forward, before he got it under control. He turned in his seat, his face red from fright at her shouting.

And the pyramid sign, slowly and still revolving gracefully, fell from the roof of the hotel to crash to earth where they had been just seconds before.

Level A

1. Why was Julia so tired? _____

_____

2. Why didn't Julia's parents hear her crying in the night? _____

_____

3. How long had Julia and her parents been on holiday? _____

_____

4. In Julia's dream, what does the rope represent? _____

_____

Level B

1. In your own words, explain the sentence: 'Something about it stabbed Julia's heart with an icy knife.'.

_____

_____

_____

2. What do you think might have happened if Julia hadn't had her dream? _____

_____

_____

3. Imagine Julia told her mother about her dream. What do you think her mother would have said?

_____

_____

_____

4. How could Julia keep tearing at the rope even though she was hurting her hands?

_____

_____

Level C

1. How appropriate is the title of the story? Why? What else could it be called?

   _____

   _____

   _____

2. How old do you think Julia is? _____ What makes you think this?

   _____

   _____

   _____

3. The writer doesn't explain Julia's dream, but leaves it to you to work out. How successful is this? Explain.

   _____

   _____

   _____

4. Imagine you are Julia. A television news team is reporting the event. How will you explain your dream to them? Write down the questions they might ask and the answers you would give.

   _____

   _____

   _____

   _____

   _____

   _____

   _____

   _____

   _____

   _____

Are We The First?

If we accept scientific theory, the earth is many, many millions of years old. Yet humans have only been on it for a very short time. Or have they? People who believe that this is not the first time the earth has been populated by 'humans', like to point out the following strange 'facts'. (Those who don't believe this theory simply say that these 'facts' are untrue, or can be easily explained as normal.)

1. A footprint was found in limestone in Pershing County, Nevada (USA). It shows the sole of a shoe, and is so clear you can see the rows of double stitching. Yet the rock the footprint is in is dated at 400 000 000 years old!

2. A strange bell-shaped container, shaped a bit like a school bell, and patterned with flowers made from pure silver, was dynamited out of solid rock four metres below the ground in Massachusetts in 1851! It was reported in the *Scientific American* magazine.

3. In 1928 in Oklahoma, a miner in a coal mine, after firing explosives to break up the coal, discovered a wall made of polished concrete blocks about 30 centimetres square. This was approximately 3 000 metres underground!

4. Manuscripts many thousands of years old, translated in Mysore (India) in 1952, included a design for the construction of a vertical-flight transport aircraft (like a helicopter with wings) for carrying ammunition, as well as the plans for passenger planes that could carry up to 500 people!

5. Two skulls dated at 3 500 years old, found in Armenia (Europe) in 1972, showed that the women, when alive, had undergone brain surgery of the most delicate kind, involving boring into the skull and then plugging the wound with shaped animal bone—and had lived for up to 15 years after the successful operation!

6. Ruins of ancient buildings in Scotland, Turkey and Arabia have been discovered where so much heat has been applied to them some time in the past that bricks and skeletons have turned to carbon, sand has turned to glass, and even the rocks have melted and flowed like water. Today, such heat is only known in a nuclear explosion!

7. An African tribe (the Dogon), as part of their folklore which has been handed down from generation to generation for thousands of years, tell how Sirius is actually a double star, that its invisible other half is 'the heaviest of all stars' and that it revolves around Sirius once every fifty years. It wasn't until 1862 that modern scientists discovered that Sirius *does* have another partner, which *does* revolve once every fifty years around Sirius and that, because it is a white dwarf star, this partner is *extremely* heavy for its relatively small size! But how did a 'primitive' African tribe know this?

There are many cases such as these. In fact, whole books have been written on them and films made about them. Much of what is claimed can be disproved very easily as just wild imagination. But there are some things that, while they may not prove anything, are just too weird and mysterious to be easily explained!

Level A

1. How deep was the wall of concrete blocks beneath the earth?

   _____

2. Which African tribe knows all about Sirius? _____

3. True or false?: The stories in the article are all true. _____

4. What do you need to turn sand to glass?

   _____

   _____

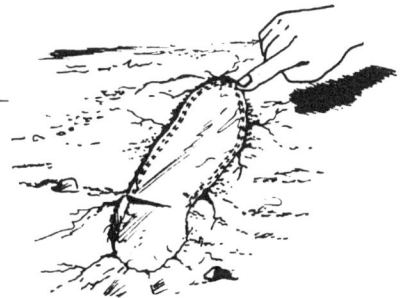

5. Where may have the first brain surgery occurred?

   _____

   _____

Level B

1. In one sentence, write in your own words the main idea of the article.

   _____

   _____

2. What's so strange about finding the plans for aircraft in India? _____

   _____

   _____

3. Why do you think it is important to mention that the bell-shaped container was reported in the *Scientific American* magazine?

   _____

   _____

4. Give a 'normal' explanation for the footprints in the limestone. _____

   _____

   _____

   _____

Level C

1. In just one article, the writer uses an exclamation mark eight times! Explain why this might be.

   _____

   _____

2. Look at any three of the seven strange 'facts'. How would you prove or disprove them?

   _____

   _____

   _____

   _____

   _____

   _____

3. What do you think—are we the first? Why? _____

   _____

   _____

   _____

   _____

4. In a paragraph or two, tell the story of finding the underground concrete blocks from the miner's point of view.

   _____

   _____

   _____

   _____

   _____

   _____

   _____

Tunguska

Just after 7.00 a.m. on 30 June 1908, an enormous explosion occurred over an extremely remote area near the Stony Tunguska River in what was then called Russia. Although it was nearly 20 years later before the actual site was examined, there were many eyewitnesses to the explosion. Their reports were startling!

They told how a cigar-shaped object, as bright as the sun and trailing smoke, raced across the sky with a deafening roar, before exploding into a pillar of fire and mushroom-shaped cloud of black smoke that reached some 20 kilometres high! Scientists later calculated the force of that explosion as equal to somewhere around 35 000 000 tonnes of TNT! (This makes it as large as the largest hydrogen bomb explosion.)

The blast was so large that the shock waves from it travelled twice around the earth through the atmosphere before fading away. Seismic waves ('earthquake' waves) were detected as far away as Washington, DC (USA). It also caused the sky to glow strangely at night; people in London actually panicked because the nights were so bright, while closer to the blast it was possible to take photographs at midnight—without a flash!

In 1927, a Russian professor finally reached Tunguska with a team of scientists. He found an area of devastation of almost 2 000 square kilometres, where trees and all vegetation had been flattened and incinerated black. Their roots all pointed to the centre of the blast. The professor investigated further, expecting to find a huge meteorite crater. To his surprise, there was no crater, just a number of small holes a few metres across. What on earth had caused the explosion then, if not a meteorite?

It wasn't until much later, after World War II, that scientists recognised the effects as being the same as those to be found after an aerial nuclear explosion! But Tunguska happened more than 30 years *before* the first atomic bombs were invented!

Then came the most controversial explanation of all—that the strange object had been a damaged alien spacecraft and the explosion had been caused when its nuclear-powered engine detonated. At first, this explanation was rubbished by everyone. But when the statements by the eyewitnesses were examined, researchers were surprised to find that the object had made several sharp course changes before exploding—*as though it was being controlled!* This was something a meteorite did *not* do.

Today, however, it is generally accepted that the Tunguska explosion *was* caused by a special type of meteorite—but this still can not be proved. Until it *is* proved, it must remain a possibility that it just *could* have been some sort of alien spacecraft. What do you think?

Level A

1.   Why was it possible to take photographs at midnight near Tunguska in 1908?

_____

_____

2.   Why didn't scientists at first recognise the blast effects were the same as those of an aerial nuclear explosion?

_____

_____

3.   Apart from a meteorite, what did some people think caused the explosion?

_____

_____

4.   True or false?:

Meteorites often make sharp turns in the atmosphere before exploding. _____

Level B

1.   Why did the roots of the trees all point to the centre of the blast? _____

_____

_____

2.   If all this took place in an extremely remote area of Russia, how is it that the exact date and time of the explosion are known?

_____

3.   Why is it possible that the eyewitnesses' stories may not have been 100% reliable?

_____

_____

4.   If it was suddenly proved that the explosion was an alien spaceship, what effect would it have on science and scientists?

_____

_____

Level C

1.　What do you feel the writer believes happened at Tunguska? Why? _____

_____

_____

_____

2.　Why were the eyewitness reports 'startling'? _____

_____

_____

3.　Many people would *like* to believe the Tunguska explosion was caused by a spaceship.
　　Why do you think this might be?

_____

_____

_____

4.　You are an eyewitness to the Tunguska explosion. Write down your story for a newspaper
　　report.

_____	_____
_____	_____
_____	_____
_____	_____
_____	_____
_____	_____
_____	_____
_____	_____
_____	Story by
_____	_____

Asking Directions

When Leigh had decided to cycle home from her best friend Maria's place, she hadn't been nervous. After all, she had lived in the country all her life, she was 12 years old and certainly not afraid of the dark, and it was only a 20-minute ride home anyway. But halfway home, when she couldn't see the lights of either farmhouse, she began to wish she hadn't been quite so brave, and had accepted a ride home from Mr Zampatti. She pedalled faster.

She went round a slight bend in the gravel road, where the oak trees crowded, seeming to reach for her in the pale moonlight—and it suddenly got cold—very cold! There was a thick white fog, hanging in layers above the road, and misting the top branches of the trees. Leigh's breath puffed in thick clouds in front of her, and her bare legs were so cold they felt like they were burning.

Her heart was thumping loudly and she was panting as she pedalled away at top speed, so that she didn't hear the car until it suddenly appeared beside her like a silent black ghost. She squealed to herself and skidded to a stop. The big black limousine also stopped, the brake lights glowing bright red in the mist. The gravel scrunched as it reversed down the road to Leigh. She thought it was the quietest car she had ever heard—or not heard.

The car stopped alongside her. She tried to look inside, but the windows were tinted almost black and she could see nothing. Then the window on the passenger's side began to slide silently down—and Leigh found she was holding her breath, too frightened even to move!

In the soft glow of the many instruments, Leigh saw something move inside. Then a very bright light suddenly clicked on, and Leigh found herself staring at—a little grey-haired old lady! The relief was so great, Leigh almost burst into giggles—or tears. But she managed to control herself.

'Hello, dear,' said the little old lady. 'Can you help me? I'm afraid I'm lost. Can you tell me where I might find the nearest airport? It's very important. I have to be there in the next five minutes.'

'Airport? I'll say you're lost,' Leigh said, getting off her bike and walking closer to the car. She could feel a strange tingle coming from it, like static electricity. 'You have to go back down this road the way you've just come for about 10 miles. Then, when the road forks, take the left fork for another 10 or so miles. That puts you back on the main road. Then you turn right and follow the signs for about another 20 miles. I'm afraid there's no way you're going to make it in the next five minutes though!'

'Thank you very much, dear; you're very kind to an old lady. And don't worry; I'll make it in plenty of time.'

The window wound up again and the car moved off. A little way ahead, it did a three-point turn and came back. The headlights flashed as it went past Leigh, and she smiled and waved. Poor old dear, she thought. She hasn't got a chance. She turned to give a final wave—and froze.

The car was changing. First the colour was fading—from black to a silvery-grey. While that was happening, the wheels were disappearing into the arches, though the car kept going forward, floating above the ground. Then the big, round red tail-lights began to grow, until they were the size of dustbin lids, glowing more and more brightly all the while.

Then the 'car' lifted into the dark sky and, with a faint whistling sound, was gone faster than the eye could follow.

Level A

1. What was Maria's surname?

2. How far was the 'car' from the airport?

3. What made Leigh hold her breath, 'too frightened even to move'?

4. Why did Leigh feel like laughing—or crying?

Level B

1. Is it important that it suddenly got very cold? Why?

2. Why does the writer describe the car as a 'silent black ghost'?

3. What clues does the writer give you during the story that the car is not all it seems to be?

4. What do you think Leigh did after the 'car' took off?

Level C

1. At what point in the story does it move from reality to fantasy? _____

    _____

2. 'Asking Directions' is a very down-to-earth title. For what reasons do you think the writer chose this title? What else might it have been called?

    _____

    _____

    _____

3. Why would the writer make the driver of the car a 'little grey-haired old lady'?

    _____

    _____

4. Put yourself in Leigh's shoes. In a paragraph or two, explain to your parents what has just happened to you in a way that will make them believe your story!

    _____

    _____

    _____

    _____

    _____

    _____

    _____

    _____

    _____

    _____

    _____

    _____

    _____

    _____

    _____

Answers

SPECIAL NOTE:
Only Level A questions are literal; the remainder all require a certain amount of interpretation. Hence, only Level A questions can have 'right' or 'wrong' answers.

The validity of answers to questions in Levels B and C will be left to individual teachers and/or pupils to determine.

1-3 A Little Bit Wild
Level A
1. 3 500 years
2. For food on the way to 'heaven'
3. They dump them
4. It is its own boss.

4-6 Old, Old Insects
Level A
1. Coal and rock
2. 300 000 000 years
3. (Just about) anything!
4. Most can fly. Make themselves flat to sneak in anywhere. Can go from stopped to full speed fasther than a sports car. Very hard to kill

7-9 Eye's in the NIight
Level A
1. To get a drink of water
2. A monster/snake
3. Yellow

10-12 A Real Australian
Level A
1. Its tail
2. A joey
3. It never stops growing
4. Dry grasslands of Australia

13-15 The First Pets
Level A
1. dog
2. More than 400
3. About 10 000 years
4. Hunting, herding, pets

16-18 What a Whopper
Level A
1. Blue Whale
2. Shrimp-like animals
3. Up to four tonnes
4. Hot breath - water vapour

19-21
Wings of Fire
Level A
1. parrots
2. White - landing guide
3. They were frightened (by the men and machines)

22-24 The Speed Champion
Level A
1. Falcon
2. False
3. Larger
4. Dive 240 k/hr
5. It hits its pray in the back of the head with claws

25-27 Boats 'n' Things that Float
Level A
1. Rust
2. Sails
3. Timber (wood)
4. Aluminium and fibreglass

28-30 A Tall Tale!
Level A
1. On the weekend
2. Grandad lost the wedding ring she had given him
3. His false teeth shot out and went over the side
4. Grandad's wedding ring

31-33 Danger! Beware!
Level A
1. They inject their poison
2. You'll get stung more!
3. They are camouflaged
4. Scorpionfish

34-36 Fishing: For and Against
Level A
1. To eat
2. They spend lots of money (or similar)
3. A sport where an animal dies
4. There wil be no fish left

37-39 Green is Not a Funny Colour
Level A
1. Seasick(ness)
2. Ears
3. A couple of days
4. The medicine is released slowly into the bloodstream (or similar)
5. Mal de mar - France

40-42 Shark!
Level A
1. So more people could see him: To show off
2. Kevin
3. Leo
4. Uncle Pete: man in petrol station: man at launching ramp

43-45 How About the Future?
Level A
1. Carrying goods beneath the ocean (or similar)
2. Running out of dry land (or similar)
3. The water around them
4. To replace 'natural' fish: for food (or similar)

46-48 What's for Dinner?
Level A
1. It was so dark where they lived
2. Fish
3. Finetta and Finelder
4. False (About twice the size of the submarine)

49-51 Atlantis—Lost or Found?
Level A
1. Atlanteans
2. Atlantic
3. They found a buried civilisation unlike any other
4. The Bermuda Triangle

52-54 A Strange Triangle
Level A
1. Because of the reported strange happenings there
2. Compass deflection/time and/or visual distortion
3. *Marie Celeste*
4. Female (... *still thinking she was lost.*)

55-57 Batteries Included
Level A
1. Lissie. Kylie calls her that.
2. Two
3. Head teacher
4. No coffee or tea in the staffroom/just sat there/ did not speak/no one spoke to her

58-60 'I Want to Drink Your Blood'
Level A
1. Three years
2. The 'body' had a heartbeat
3. No. It gives reasons against the belief in their reality.
4. Mistaken identity/Ignorance (mistakenly declared dead)

61-63 They Just Disappeared
Level A
1. About 65 000 000 years
2. False. No humans on earth then.
3. Meteorite strike/cooling down of earth
4. It could be underwater

64-66 Premonition
Level A
1. Her dream woke her up every night
2. She had a separate room
3. A week
4. The car seatbelt (Something holding her back)

67-69 Are We The First?
Level A
1. (Approximately) 3 000 metres
2. The Dogon
3. False (No proof is given)
4. Extreme heat
5. Armenia (Europe)

70-72 Tunguska
Level A
1. Because of the glow in the sky
2. Because in 1908 they didn't have nuclear explosions!
3. An exploding spaceship
4. False

73-75 Asking Directions
Level A
1. Zampatti
2. About 40 miles
3. The car and the window sliding down
4. Relief (at seeing just a little grey-haired lady in the car)